Whoa!

By Cameron Carleton

Co-Created by David & Carissa Carleton

Disclaimer: The information contained in this book was true at the time of publication.

Copyright © 2022 Cameron Carleton

All rights reserved.

Paperback ISBN: 978-1-7386954-0-9
Ebook ISBN: 978-1-7386954-1-6

First paperback edition August 2022.

Co-created by David Carleton and Carissa Carleton
Illustrated by Carissa Carleton

Hey friends! Want to know something cool?

Sure!

Did you know that owls can turn their heads *very* far around?

Like this?

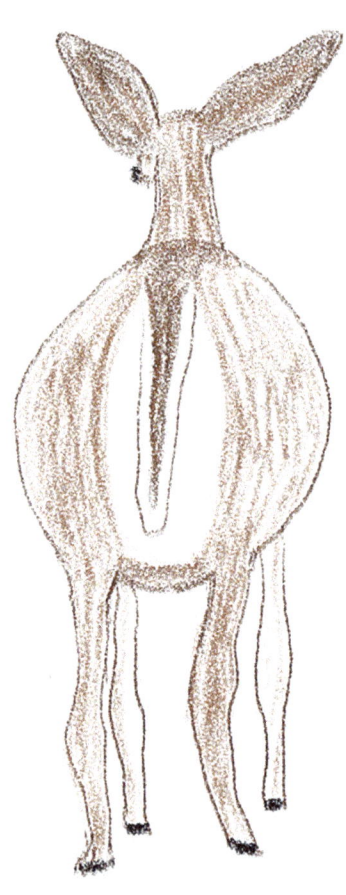

No.

Like this?

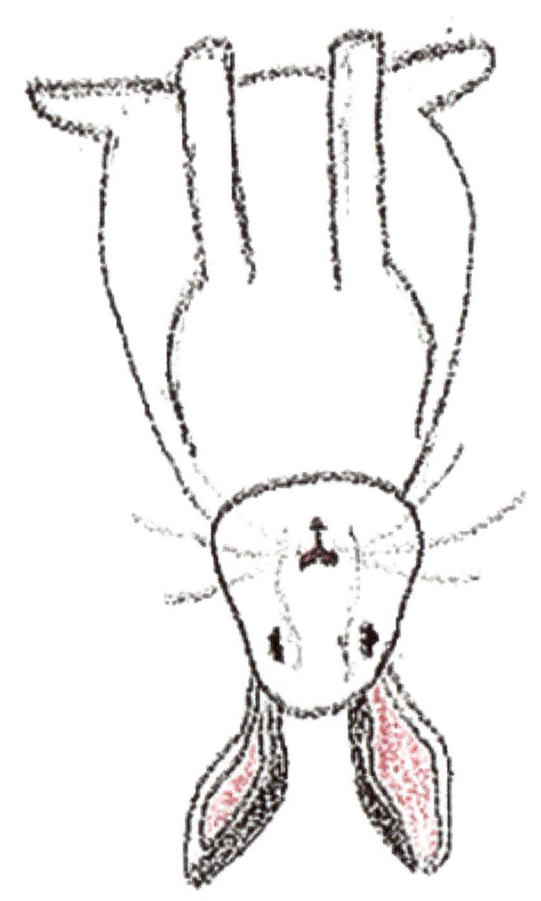

No.

Like this!

Whoa!

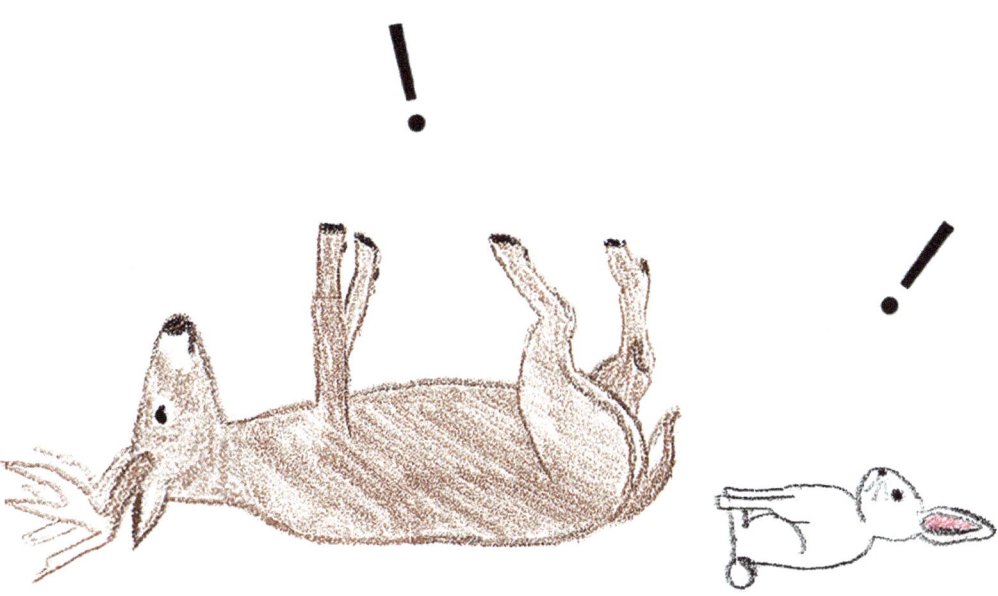

Did you know that rabbits can have *many* babies every year?

Like this?

No.

Like this?

Like this.

Whoa!

Did you know that deer can regrow their antlers *every* year?

Like this?

No.

Like this?

No.

Like

This!

Whoa!

CAM'S FACTS

OWLS

Owls can't move their eyes back and forth to look around like humans can. Instead, they rely on their flexible necks to turn their heads around by more than 180 degrees. That's more than half of a circle! Their heads can turn to look directly behind them.

RABBITS

Rabbits can have litters of up to 7 babies (called kittens). They can do this up to 5 times per year. That means a rabbit can have 35 babies in a year!

DEER

Most deer shed and regrow their antlers every year. Their antlers are covered in "velvet", which eventually dies. After mating season, the deer rub their antlers on branches to remove them. In the spring, the antlers begin to grow back.

www.ingramcontent.com/pod-product-compliance
Lightning Source LLC
Chambersburg PA
CBHW051321110526
44590CB00031B/4433